ICAEW
Audit and Assurance

CW00546258

First edition 2007, Fifteenth edition 2021

ISBN 9781 5097 3847 2

British Library Cataloguing-in-Publication Data

A catalogue record for this book is available from the
British Library

Published by

BPP Learning Media Ltd
BPP House, Aldine Place
142-144 Uxbridge Road
London W12 8AA

www.bpp.com/learningmedia

Printed in the United Kingdom

Your learning materials, published by BPP Learning Media
Ltd, are printed on paper obtained from traceable
sustainable sources.

The content of this publication is intended to prepare
students for the ICAEW examinations, and should not be
used as professional advice. Although every effort has
been made to ensure that the contents of this book are
correct at the time of going to press, BPP Learning Media
makes no warranty that the information in this book is
accurate or complete and accepts no liability for any loss
or damage suffered by any person acting or refraining
from acting as a result of the material in this book.

ICAEW takes no responsibility for the content of any
supplemental training materials supplied by the Partner
in Learning.

The ICAEW Partner in Learning logo, ACA and ICAEW
CFAB are all registered trademarks of ICAEW and are
used under licence by BPP Learning Media Ltd.

Welcome to BPP Learning Media's **Passcards** for ICAEW **Audit and Assurance**.

- They **save you time**. Important topics are summarised for you.
- They incorporate **diagrams** to kick start your memory.
- They follow the overall **structure** of the ICAEW Workbook, but BPP Learning Media's ICAEW **Passcards** are not just a condensed book. Each card has been separately designed for clear presentation. Topics are self-contained and can be grasped visually.
- ICAEW **Passcards** are **just the right size** for pockets, briefcases and bags.
- ICAEW **Passcards focus on the exams** you will be facing.

Run through the **Passcards** as often as you can during your final revision period. The day before the exam, try to go through the **Passcards** again! You will then be well on your way to passing your exams.

Good luck!

Preface
Contents

1: Reintroduction to audit and assurance

Topic List

Assurance

Audit

Audit and assurance compared

This chapter provides an introduction into why there is a need for assurance services, for example, audit and review. It is important that you have grasped the key auditing concepts outlined in this chapter because it is the foundation for success in this exam.

| Assurance | Audit | Audit and assurance compared |

Assurance engagement: an engagement in which a practitioner aims to obtain sufficient appropriate audit evidence in order to express a conclusion designed to enhance the degree of confidence of the intended users other than the responsible party about the subject matter information (that is, the outcome of the measurement or evaluation of an underlying subject matter against criteria).

Elements

- Responsible party
- Practitioner
- User of the report
- Subject matter
- Criteria
- Evidence to support conclusion
- Written report containing conclusion

Benefits

- Enhances credibility of information
- Reduces risk of management bias, error or fraud
- Draws attention to any deficiencies
- Professional, objective, unbiased opinion

Levels of assurance

Assurance type	Assurance level	Opinion/conclusion	Example
Reasonable	High	Positive	Audit of financial information
Limited	Moderate	Negative	Review of financial information

The type of engagement needs to be specified in the terms of engagement.

Remember that no report on an assurance engagement can ever provide absolute assurance, because of the nature of the evidence available.

Audit of financial statements: the auditor's objective is to obtain reasonable assurance about whether the financial statements as a whole are free from material misstatement, whether due to fraud or error.

Auditor's opinion: the opinion expressed by the auditor when they conclude whether the financial statements are prepared, in all material respects, in accordance with an applicable financial reporting framework.

An audit fits the criteria of an assurance engagement because it has:

(1) Three party involvement:
- Shareholders (users)
- Directors (responsible party)
- Audit firm (practitioner)

(2) Subject matter – the financial statements

(3) Relevant criteria – law and accounting standards

(4) Evidence – sufficient and appropriate

(5) Report – written in a prescribed format

The audit threshold

In the UK, small companies (as defined by the Companies Act 2006) are exempt from audit if they can satisfy two out of the three following criteria:

- Turnover does not exceed £10.2 million
- Balance sheet total does not exceed £5.1 million
- Number of employees does not exceed 50

Audit and assurance compared | Audit | Assurance

Nature of work undertaken

Audit ISA (UK) 500	Review of FS ISRE 2400	Examining prospective financial information ISAE 3400
■ Inspection ■ Observation ■ External confirmation ■ Recalculation ■ Reperformance ■ Analytical procedures ■ Inquiry	■ Inquiry eg, into the accounting principles in place ■ Analytical procedures eg, comparison with prior periods	■ Assessment of assumptions ■ Recomputation ■ Written representations

2: Responsibilities

Topic List

Respective responsibilities

Fraud and error

Related parties

Laws and regulations

Money laundering

Expectations gap

The primary responsibility of the statutory auditor is to report to the shareholders on the truth and fairness of the financial statements.

Responsibilities are determined by legislation, standards and the terms of engagement.

Management

- Managing the business so as to achieve its objectives
- Assessing business risks
- Safeguarding assets
- Keeping proper accounting records
- Preparing financial statements
- Compliance with laws and regulations

Statutory auditor

- Form an independent opinion on the truth and fairness of the financial statements
- Confirm that they have been properly prepared in accordance with Companies Act 2006
- Confirm that directors' report and strategic report are consistent with FS

Management cannot delegate any of its responsibilities to the external auditor.

Fraud for audit purposes can mean:

- Fraudulent financial reporting
- Misappropriation of assets

The responsibility for preventing and detecting fraud rests with those charged with governance and management.

ISA (UK) 240 states that the auditor must obtain reasonable assurance that FS are free from material misstatement, whether caused by fraud or error.

An **error** is an unintentional misstatement. Auditors should design procedures that are capable of detecting errors. Errors could give rise to material misstatements in the FS.

Exam focus

Look for **factors** in questions which might indicate a **risk** of fraud. These could include:

- Management with poor integrity
- Deficient internal control components
- Unusual transactions
- Financial reporting pressures
- Problems in gaining sufficient appropriate audit evidence
- Unique issues arising from systems

ISA (UK) 550

The auditor shall perform audit procedures and related activities to obtain information relevant to identify the risks of material misstatement associated with related party relationships and transactions.

Issues

- Related parties may have an undue influence on the entity being audited
- Transactions may not be carried out on arm's length terms
- Risk of non-disclosure

Audit work required at

- Planning stage
- Detailed work stage
- Review stage

Planning

- Consider materiality by reference to the related party

Detailed testing

- Obtain full list of related parties
- Ensure whole audit team aware
- Audit evidence may be limited

Review

- Written representations

The **auditor's responsibilities** for considering laws and regulations as part of the audit is discussed in ISA (UK) 250 Section A *Consideration of Laws and Regulations in an Audit of Financial Statements*.

- **Plan**

  Understand the legal framework and assess risk of non-compliance

- **Evidence**

  Inquiry and written representations from management and those charged with governance

- **Document findings**

  Consider impact of non-compliance on audit opinion

Management is responsible for ensuring that laws and regulations are complied with.

Reporting non-compliance

Those charged with governance

- Non-compliance shall be communicated to those charged with governance

Shareholders

- Consider the impact on auditor's report and report accordingly

Third parties

- Is there a statutory duty?
- Is it in the public interest?
- Obtain legal advice

Respective responsibilities	Fraud and error	Laws and regulations	Related parties	Money laundering	Expectations gap

Money laundering: the process by which criminals attempt to conceal the true origin and ownership of the proceeds of their criminal activity, allowing them to maintain control over the proceeds and, ultimately, providing a legitimate cover for their sources of income.

Criminal offences in the UK

- Possessing, dealing with or concealing the proceeds of any crime
- Attempting, assisting or incitement to commit money laundering
- Failure of an individual in the regulated sector to report a suspicion of money laundering
- Tipping-off

UK Money Laundering Regulations

- Appoint a ML Compliance Principal (MLCP) and an ML Reporting Officer (MLRO)
- Undertake customer due diligence
- Report suspicion of money laundering without 'tipping off'
- Maintain specific records
- Put policies in place to ensure continued compliance with the regulations
- Train staff in all these issues

Expectations gap: the gap between the expectations of users of assurance reports and the auditor's statutory responsibilities.

Common misconceptions

- The auditor is responsible for preparing the FS
- The auditor is responsible for detecting fraud
- The auditor checks all transactions (failure to grasp materiality)
- A 'clean' auditor's report means the FS are 'correct'

Narrowing the gap

- Auditor's report sets out responsibilities of directors
- Auditor's report sets out responsibilities of auditor
- Auditor's report explains how an audit is conducted (test basis, materiality, etc)
- Role of audit committee in corporate governance

Why things still go wrong

- Companies still fail
- Fraud is committed
- Genuine mistakes are made
- Audit failure can occur, either through no fault or through negligence

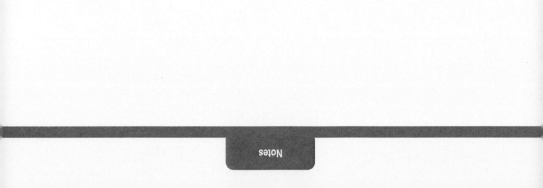
Notes

3: Professional standards

This chapter looks at the regulatory environment in which auditing takes place. The basic duties of auditors are established by law but detailed professional standards are required to ensure that audits are carried out to a consistent quality.

Directors need to ensure that internal controls perform effectively, as part of their statutory duties.

| International standards on auditing | The Financial Reporting Council (FRC) | Internal control effectiveness |

IFAC is the International Federation of Accountants, based in New York.

The International Auditing and Assurance Standards Board (elected from members of the IFAC) issues **International Standards on Auditing** (ISAs). ISAs are specially written to try to incorporate the differences which exist between the accounting requirements of various national laws.

They do not override national law, but if national law conflicts with the best practice in an ISA, member bodies of IFAC from that country are required to encourage a change in the law to conform to the ISA.

IFAC co-operates with member bodies from around the world to initiate, co-ordinate and guide efforts to achieve international technical, ethical and educational pronouncements for the accountancy profession. Members of IFAC automatically become members of the international accounting standards body.

ISAs

- Contain:

  - Basic principles and essential procedures
  - Explanatory and other material

  Basic principles and essential procedures are interpreted in the context of the explanatory and other material.

- It is necessary to consider the whole text of the ISA.
- In exceptional circumstances departure from ISAs may be required to achieve audit objectives.

International standards on auditing | **The Financial Reporting Council (FRC)** | Internal control effectiveness

The FRC issues a number of pronouncements, including:

ISAs (UK)

Form
Based on IAASB's ISAs augmented by extra sections on UK issues where necessary.

Authority
Auditors face discipline from their RSB if they do not comply.
Compliance will be considered in court.

Practice notes
These assist the auditor in applying ISAs (UK) of general application.

- Persuasive, not prescriptive
- Indicative of good practice
- Similar to ISAs explanatory material

Bulletins
These provide auditors with timely guidance on new and emerging issues.

Ethical Standard
This provides guidance on potential ethical dilemmas.

Amid heavy criticism for its failure to prevent significant corporate collapses, the FRC is set to be disbanded and replaced with a new body called the Audit, Reporting and Governance Authority (ARGA).

Directors

Internal controls and risk management are very important in fulfiling directors' duties to the shareholders, which are:

- To safeguard the assets
- To prevent and detect fraud

Protect the investment of the shareholder

Therefore they:

- Set up a system of internal control
- Review its effectiveness
- Consider the need for internal audit

Auditors

As part of their audit:

- Ascertain controls
- Review controls
- Evaluate controls
- Determine audit approach based on controls

Can also offer services to provide assurance separate from audit:

- Review design of internal control system
- Review operation of internal control system

Notes

4: Professional ethics

Ethics is a key topic area.

When approaching questions on ethics, follow a three-stage strategy:

- *What do the fundamental principles say?*

- *What does the detailed guidance say?*

- *What does my common sense/practical experience tell me?*

Code of Ethics

Integrity	To be straightforward and honest in all professional and business relationships.
Objectivity	Not to compromise professional or business judgements because of bias, conflict of interest or undue influence of others.
Professional competence and due care	To: (i) Attain and maintain professional knowledge and skill at the level required to ensure that a client or employing organisation receives competent professional service, based on current technical and professional standards, and relevant legislation; and (ii) Act diligently and in accordance with applicable technical and professional standards.
Confidentiality	To respect the confidentiality of information acquired as a result of professional and business relationships.
Professional behaviour	To comply with relevant laws and regulations and avoid any conduct that the professional accountant knows or should know might discredit the profession.

IESBA Code of ethics	Threats to independence	Safeguards	Independence	Confidentiality	Areas of controversy

Compliance with the fundamental principles may potentially be threatened by a broad range of circumstances:

Threats	
■ **Self-interest** threat	Financial interests, incentive compensation arrangements, undue dependence on fees
■ **Self-review** threat	Data being reviewed by the same person responsible for preparing it
■ **Advocacy** threat	Acting as an advocate on behalf of an assurance client in litigation or disputes with third parties
■ **Familiarity** threat	Former partner of the firm being a director or officer of the client
■ **Intimidation** threat	Threat of dismissal or replacement, being pressured to reduce inappropriately the extent of work performed in order to reduce fees
■ **Management** threat	Making judgements and decisions which are the responsibility of management

Three categories of safeguards exist: those created by regulations, those created by the individual and those created in the work environment.

Regulations

- ICAEW Code/IESBA Code/FRC ES
- ISAs (UK)

Individual

- Complying with continuing professional development requirements
- Keeping records of contentious issues and decisions
- Using an independent mentor
- Maintaining contact with legal advisers and professional bodies

Work environment

- Recruitment procedures
- Appropriate disciplinary processes
- Leadership that stresses the importance of ethical behaviour
- Policies and procedures to implement and monitor the
    - Quality of employee performance
    - Quality control of engagements
- Using different partners and teams for the provision of non-audit services to assurance clients
- Discussing ethical issues with those charged with governance
- Consultation with another professional accountant

Independence

Independence of mind is the state of mind that permits the provision of an opinion without being affected by influences that compromise professional judgement, allowing an individual to act with integrity, and exercise objectivity and professional scepticism.

Independence in appearance is the avoidance of facts and circumstances that are so significant that a reasonable and informed third party, having knowledge of all relevant information, including safeguards applied, would reasonably conclude a firm's, or a team member's, integrity, objectivity or professional scepticism had been compromised.

Aims to help firms and members.

1. Identify threats to independence

2. Evaluate significance of threats

3. Identify and apply safeguards to reduce threats to an acceptable level

Example

A key risk arises from the provision of other services to audit clients. An auditor:

- Should not take on the responsibilities of management
- May not prepare accounts for a public interest entity (eg, a plc)
- Must not review their own work
- Cannot be an employee of an audit client

Safeguards against loss of objectivity

- Quality control procedures
- Audit committee _____
- Audit rotation _____

Is a requirement for listed companies in the UK and is widely recommended for other companies. It is a committee of at least three non-executive directors (two for small companies).

Advantages

- To auditor: independent liaison between executive directors and themselves
- To company: can help give increased confidence in transparency of reporting

Is where clients change auditors on a regular basis (say every five years).

The benefit of audit rotation is that loss of independence through familiarity is guarded against. In practice audit rotation is not popular because of the high recurring costs of first audits, loss of trust and experience built up, and internal rotation by the audit firm.

| IESBA *Code of* *ethics* | Threats to independence | Safeguards | Independence | **Confidentiality** | Areas of controversy |

Accountants owe their clients a **professional duty of confidentiality**, except in the following situations.

Obligatory disclosure

If a member knows or suspects his client to have committed a **terrorist offence**, an offence of **treason** or a **money laundering** offence he is obliged to disclose all the information at his disposal to a competent authority. In the UK, he is required to report a suspicion of money laundering. Local legislation may also require auditors to disclose other infringements.

Voluntary disclosure

In certain cases voluntary disclosure may be made by the member where:

- To comply with the quality review of ICAEW or another professional body;
- To respond to an inquiry or investigation by ICAEW or another professional or regulatory body;
- To protect the professional interests of a professional accountant in legal proceedings; or
- To comply with technical and professional standards, including ethics requirements.

Areas of controversy include:

- Multiple services:
  - Problems can be overcome by using different teams of staff and ensuring that the engagement letter identifies other work separately.

- Opinion shopping:
  - Where a client seeks a second opinion from other auditors, there is a professional duty for the other auditor to seek permission to communicate with the first auditors.

- Conflict of interest:
  - Can be avoided by using information barriers, making full disclosure or not accepting the appointment.

5: Quality control

Probably the most important consideration in practice management is quality control. This chapter covers the specific guidance in relation to quality practice and procedures: ISA (UK) 220, Quality Control for an Audit of Financial Statements and ISQC (UK) 1, Quality Control for Firms that Perform Audits and Reviews of Financial Statements and other Assurance and Related Services Engagements.

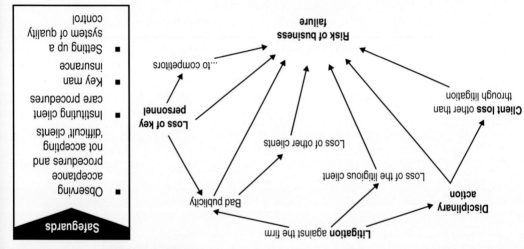

Quality control: firm level

Quality control: individual audit

The firm shall establish and maintain a system of quality control and shall document its policies and procedures.

In addition to the following the QC system shall include procedures for the acceptance of engagements and to ensure that ethical requirements are met.

Leadership responsibilities

- Sufficient and appropriate experience
- Ability to carry out the job
- Authority to carry out the job

Human resources

- Recruitment
- Capabilities
- Career development
- Compensation
- Performance evaluation
- Competence
- Promotion
- Estimation of personnel needs

Monitoring

QC procedures must be:
- Relevant
- Adequate
- Operating effectively
- Complied with

Corrective action includes:
- Remedial action with individual.
- Communication with training dept.
- Changes in QC policies and procedures
- Disciplinary action (if necessary)

Assignment of engagement teams

This is the responsibility of the engagement partner.

Engagement performance

This involves:
- Direction
- Supervision
- Review
- Consultation
- Resolution of disputes

The firm must also have standards as to what constitutes a suitable **quality control review**.

ISA (UK) 220, *Quality Control for an Audit of Financial Statements* applies the general principles of ISQC (UK) 1 to individual audits.

Individual audits

- Leadership – engagement partner responsible
- Adhering to professional requirements (independence and objectivity)
- Acceptance/continuance of audit
- Appropriately qualified/ experienced staff
- Engagement performance
- Monitoring QC procedures

Engagement performance

- **Direction**. Informing staff about:
  - The work to do
  - Nature of client
  - Potential problems
  - Responsibilities
- **Supervision**. Overall by engagement partner but more practical supervision given within the audit team
- **Review**. Includes consideration of whether:
  - Work complies with required standards
  - Significant matters/conclusions documented
  - Evidence is sufficient and appropriate
- **Consultation**. Contentious matters must be discussed and properly reviewed
- **Quality control review**. Evaluation of:
  - Significant judgements
  - Conclusions

Quality control: firm level

Quality control: individual audit

Possible consequences of getting audit opinion wrong

- Being sued for professional negligence
- Prosecution and fines
- Disciplinary procedures from ICAEW
- Loss of reputation, clients, key staff
- Collapse of assurance firm

6: Accepting engagements

Topic List

Tendering

Risk analysis

Acceptance

Agreeing terms

Exam questions could be set in the context of a change of auditor. This could involve:

- *Ethical issues*
- *Practice management issues*

Be prepared to link issues in the syllabus when you are working through these passcards. Generally questions in the exam are scenario-based and bring in lots of different issues. Bear in mind that the professional appointment may be for a service other than audit.

Tendering | Risk analysis | Acceptance | Agreeing terms

Tendering

Approach by prospective client

↓

Firm considers if it wants the work

↓

Consider practical issues

↓

Estimate work involved/fees
- Fees
- Staff
- Location

↓

Obtain further details from client

↓

Background information · Work required

↓

Prepare proposal

Advertising

The medium used shall not reflect adversely on the member, ICAEW or the accountancy profession.

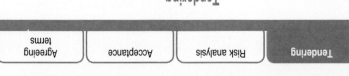

Fees

- No prescribed basis
- Percentage/contingency only for **non-assurance**
- Quoting too low a fee (lowballing) may introduce threat to competence and due care
- Fair and reasonable regarding:
  - Seniority of staff
  - Time
  - Risk/responsibility

Factors for consideration in client screening

- Management integrity
- Risk
- Relationships
- Ability to perform the work
- Engagement economics

High risk

- Poor performance
- Lack of finance
- Odd accounting
- Lack of FD
- Significant related party/ unusual transactions

Low risk

- Good prospects
- Well-financed
- Strong controls
- Prudent accounting
- Competent directors
- No unusual transactions

Sources of information about new clients

- **Enquiries** of other sources (bankers, solicitors)
- Review of **documents** (most recent annual accounts, listing particulars, credit rating)
- **Previous auditors** (previous auditors should disclose fully all relevant information)
- Review of **rules/standards** (consider specific laws/standards that relate to industry)

Before acceptance

The auditors should:

- Ensure **professionally qualified** to act → Consider whether disqualified on legal or ethical grounds
- Ensure **existing resources adequate** → Consider available time, staff and technical expertise
- Obtain **references** → Make independent enquiries if directors not personally known
- Communicate **with present auditors** → Enquire whether there are reasons/circumstances behind the change which the new auditors ought to know, also as a matter of courtesy

After acceptance

The auditors should:

- Ensure outgoing auditors' removal/resignation properly conducted
- Ensure the new auditors' appointment is valid
- Set up and submit a **letter of engagement**

Appointment decision tree

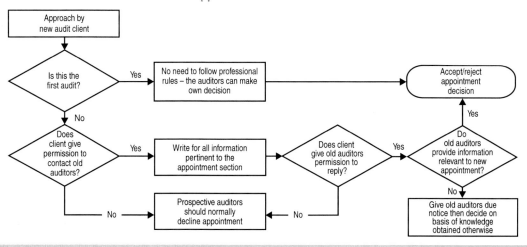

It is vital to agree terms with a client so that there is no misunderstanding as to what the service will be, to prevent problems later on. This is usually achieved through the **engagement letter**.

Items included in engagement letter

- The objective/scope of the audit (law/standards)
- Management's responsibility for the FS
- The form of any reports/communications
- Inherent limitations (risk of undiscovered misstatements)
- Arrangements regarding planning of the audit
- Expectations in relation to representations
- Basis on which the fees are computed/billing arrangements
- Any restriction of the auditors' liability where possible
- Reference to further agreements between client/auditor

7: Planning

Planning is a vital stage of the audit process and is linked to risk assessment which was introduced in the previous chapter.

The use of analytical procedures in audit planning and in other stages of the audit is also considered here.

Audit strategy

- **Scope of audit engagement**
  FR framework, industry specific requirements, expected audit coverage, availability of personnel.

- **Reporting objectives**
  Timing of audit, key dates, type and timing of reports.

- **Direction of audit**
  Materiality levels, preliminary identification of audit areas with high risk of material misstatement, evaluation of possible reliance on controls, significant business developments.

Both **internal** and **external** auditors should plan their work.

Audit plan

Auditors shall plan the audit so that the engagement will be performed in an effective manner (ISA (UK) 300).

Aim: to **reduce audit risk** to an acceptably low level:

- Description of **nature**, **timing and extent** of planned **risk assessment** procedures
- Description of **nature**, **timing and extent** of **audit procedures** at the assertion level
- Other audit procedures

Objectives of planning

- Ensure attention devoted to specific areas
- Potential problems identified
- Facilitating review

Logistics

Consider:

- Staff
- Client
- Locations
- Deadlines

Use of IT

- Consider systems at the client
- Can auditors use computers effectively?

CAATs Data analytics Admin Communication with
partner/other staff

Time budget

- Important for a cost-effective audit
- Need them to assist effective planning

Prior year   Help in risk   Remember
time records   assessment   materiality

Subsidiary objectives of the engagement

All staff need to know what the objectives are.
For example, the auditors often produce a report
to management, outlining deficiencies in internal
controls.

Remember: the primary objective is to give the audit opinion.

Overall audit plan	
Understanding the entity and its environment	■ General economic factors and industry conditions ■ Important characteristics of the client, (a) business, (b) principal business strategies, (c) financial performance, (d) reporting requirements, (plus changes since the previous audit) ■ The operating style and control consciousness of directors and management ■ The accounting and control systems and any expected changes in the period ■ ISA (UK) 315, *Identifying and Assessing the Risks of Material Misstatement* looks at gaining knowledge of the business and using it to assess risks. It requires the audit team to discuss the susceptibility of the FS to material misstatement.
Risk and materiality	■ The setting of materiality for audit planning purposes ■ The expected assessments of risks or error and identification of significant audit areas ■ Any indication that misstatements that could have a material effect on the financial statements might arise because of fraud or for any other reason ■ The identification of complex accounting areas including those involving estimates ■ ISA (UK) 330, *The Auditor's Responses to Assessed Risks* requires auditors to determine overall responses to assessed risks at the FS level (amendments to the audit team, focus on professional scepticism) and to perform procedures to respond to assessed risks at the assertion level (that is, gain sufficient, appropriate audit evidence).

Nature, timing and extent of procedures	■ The relative importance and timing of tests of control and substantive procedures (in response to assessed risks – see above)
	■ The use of information technology by the client or the auditors
	■ The use made of work of any internal audit function
	■ Procedures which need to be carried out at or before the year-end
	■ The timing of significant phases of the preparation of the financial statements
	■ The audit evidence required to reduce detection risk to an acceptably low level
Co-ordination, direction, supervision and review	■ The involvement of other auditors
	■ The involvement of experts, other third parties and internal auditors
	■ The number of locations
	■ Staffing requirements
Other matters	■ Any regulatory requirements arising from the decision to retain the engagement
	■ The possibility that the going concern basis may be inappropriate
	■ The terms of the engagement and any statutory responsibilities
	■ The nature and timing of reports or other communication with the entity that are expected under the engagement

Auditors should plan the audit work so as to perform the audit in an effective manner.

Materiality

Guidance on materiality is given in ISA (UK) 320, *Materiality in Planning and Performing an Audit*.

ISA (UK) 320

Materiality and audit risk are considered throughout the audit

Assessing materiality helps auditors to judge:

- What/how many items to test
- Whether to use sampling techniques
- Level of error leading to modification of auditor's report

These should be reassessed during the audit due to changes in accounts/risk assessments.

In order to calculate a level of materiality, the auditors will often take a range of values and use an average or weighted average.

Profit before tax
5%

Gross profit
0.5–1%

Revenue
0.5–1%

Total assets
1–2%

Net assets
2–5%

Profit after tax
5–10%

Analytical procedures

Analytical procedures consist of comparing items expected to have a relationship. Analytical procedures can be used in three ways during an audit:

- Risk assessment procedures
- Substantive procedures
- Overall review

Analytical approaches are commonly taken on:

- Business risk approach assignments
- Reviews
- Assurance engagements
- Prospective financial information

Analytical approach

Is taken in situations where:

- Auditor expects little change in figures
- Auditor has high degree of knowledge of expected changes

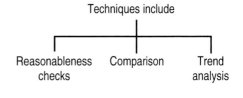

Techniques include

Reasonableness checks   Comparison   Trend analysis

TP06-8-19922-0037

ISA (UK) 570, *Going Concern* deals with the assumption of going concern as applied to FS.

Symptoms of going concern problems

Financial indications

- Withdrawal of financial support
- Adverse key financial ratios
- Inability to pay creditors on due dates

Operating indications

- Loss of key management personnel
- Labour difficulties
- Shortages of important supplies

Other indications

- Non-compliance with statutory requirements
- Pending legal proceedings for claims that cannot be satisfied
- Changes in law/regulation/government policy with potential adverse effects

| Planning | Materiality | Analytical procedures | Going concern | Risk factors |

Management override

Management has the ability to manipulate the accounting records in order to produce misleading financial statements.

Journals

Fraudulent acitivities can be perpetrated by inappropriate or unauthorised journal entries.

Revenue recognition

Auditors should be aware of the risks of material misstatements due to incorrect revenue recognition, especially where management reward is linked to revenue or profit.

Cyber security

The growth of big data and cloud computing poses new risks for businesses and auditors in relation to the security of data, particularly where it is stored online or by an external organisation.

8: Understanding the entity and its environment

Topic List

Understanding the entity

Fraud, laws and regulation

Before the auditor accepts the engagement, the firm must have a thorough understanding of the client's business.

This understanding needs to be refreshed and updated before each engagement.

Matters of which to gain understanding – from ISA (UK) 315

The entity and its environment, and the financial reporting framework

- Relevant industry, regulatory and other external factors including applicable reporting framework
- Nature of the entity
- Applicable **financial reporting framework** and **accounting policies**
- Entity's objectives and strategies and related business risks that could lead to material misstatement
- Measurement and review of the entity's financial performance
- How **inherent risk factors** affect the susceptibility to misstatement
- Entity's **system of internal control**

The entity's system of internal control

- **Control environment,** and whether this provides an appropriate foundation for the system of internal control
- Entity's **risk assessment process,** which should be appropriate to the entity's circumstances/nature/complexity
- Entity's **process to monitor** internal controls
- Entity's **information system and communication,** including the **IT environment**
- Control activities, including controls for **significant risks** and controls for **risks arising from use of IT**

Control deficiencies

- Auditor to determine whether there are any **control deficiencies**

Fraud

This includes:

- Fraudulent financial reporting
- Misappropriation of assets

Responsibilities in relation to fraud:

- **Management and those charged with governance** are responsible for prevention and detection.
- **Auditors** must be aware of the possibility of misstatement due to fraud.

ISA (UK) 240

An auditor conducting an audit in accordance with ISAs is responsible for obtaining reasonable assurance that the financial statements are free from material misstatements, whether caused by fraud or error.

Law and regulations

- Those that affect the FS indirectly but fundamentally
- Those that have a direct material effect on balances in the FS (eg, tax)

Auditors will need to assess the risk and likely impact of non-compliance.

ISA (UK) 250A

The auditor shall obtain sufficient appropriate audit evidence regarding compliance with the provisions of those laws and regulations generally recognised to have a direct effect on the determination of material amounts and disclosures in the financial statements.

Notes

9: Risk assessment

Topic List

Business risk

Audit risk

Documentation

This chapter examines the elements of audit risk, materiality and the use of analytical procedures at the audit planning stage.

Risk assessment is a key topic area and may come up in a scenario-based question where you are asked to identify risks and explain why they are risks.

Business risk is the risk inherent to the entity in its operations.

Financial risk
Risk arising from the financial activities or financial consequences of an operation.

Compliance risk
Risk that arises from non-compliance with laws and regulations.

Operational risk
Risk arising with regard to operations.

Examples of risks

- Cash flow issues
- Overtrading
- Capital issues
- Going concern
- Breakdown of accounting systems
- Credit risk
- Loss of key supplier/customer
- Loss of key employees
- Physical disasters
- Poor brand management
- Breach of law/regulation: fines
- Tax problems: fines
- Environmental law: fines/compensation

Audit risk: the risk that the auditors give an inappropriate opinion on the FS.

Audit risk = Risk of material misstatement × Detection risk

Inherent risk   ×   Control risk

Inherent risk: how likely is it that an account balance or transaction will be wrong, giving rise to a material misstatement in the FS?

Control risk: how likely is it that a misstatement will not be prevented or detected by internal controls?

Detection risk: how likely is it that audit procedures will not detect material misstatements?

ISA (UK) 315.11

The objective of the auditor is to identify and assess the risks of material misstatement, whether due to fraud or error, at the financial statement and assertion levels thereby providing a basis for designing and implementing responses to the assessed risks of material misstatement.

The auditor performs **risk assessment procedures** that allow them to assess the risks of material misstatement, and design further audit procedures (ISA 315: para. 13).

Procedures must **not** be biased towards obtaining evidence that is **corroborative**, and which excludes contradictory evidence.

The engagement team should discuss how the financial reporting framework applies, and the susceptibility to material misstatement (ISA 315: para. 17).

ISA (UK) 315

The auditor shall determine whether any of the risks identified are, in the auditor's judgement, a **significant risk**. A significant risk exists where inherent risk is close to the upper end of the spectrum of inherent risk or required to be a significant risk in accordance with an ISA.

Procedures to carry out:

- Enquiries of management/others in entity
- Analytical procedures
- Observation and inspections

They may also perform other procedures where circumstances merit it.

Audit documentation is the record of audit procedures performed, relevant audit evidence obtained and conclusions the auditor reached (also called 'working papers'). Guidance is given in ISAs (UK) 315 and 330.

Documentation

- Discussion regarding susceptibility to misstatement
- Key elements of understanding the entity
- Identified/assessed risk of material misstatement
- Risks identified/related controls evaluated
- Responses to address risk
- Nature, extent, timing of procedures
- Conclusions regarding evidence from previous audits

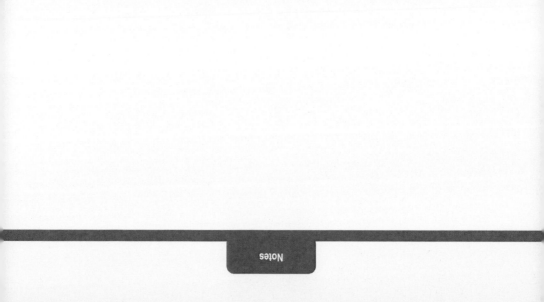

Notes

10: Audit approach

Topic List

Responding to risk assessment

Audit testing

Use of the work of others

Accounting estimates

Practical issues

In order to perform an efficient audit, it is important that the auditor has a strategy that considers the need and risks of relying on others for part of the audit evidence.

Responding to risk assessment

The auditor must formulate **an approach** to assessed risks of misstatement.

Overall responses
■ Emphasising to audit staff the need to maintain professional scepticism
■ Assigning additional or more experienced staff to the audit team
■ Using experts, the work of internal auditors or other auditors
■ Providing more supervision on the audit
■ Incorporating more unpredictability into audit procedures

Sources of audit confidence ISA (UK) 500

■ Tests of controls
■ Tests of details
■ Analytical procedures

ISA (UK) 501 provides specific guidance relating to:

■ Attendance at inventory count
■ Litigation and claims

Audit procedures

- **Inspection** of assets
- **Inspection** of documentation
- **Observation**
- **Inquiry**
- **External confirmation**
- **Recalculation/reperformance**
- **Analytical procedures**

Tests of controls

ISA (UK) 330 requires auditors to carry out tests of controls when:

- They are planning to test controls to reduce audit risk

- They are unable to derive sufficient evidence from substantive procedures

Substantive procedures

- **The auditor must always carry out substantive procedures on material items.**

- Substantive procedures constitute tests of details and/or analytical procedures.

- The use of audit data analytics enables 100% testing of a population, which has implications for the concept of controls testing.

10: Audit approach

Auditors need to obtain sufficient appropriate audit evidence to support the financial statement assertions. This is done through **substantive testing**.

Substantive procedures are tests to detect material misstatements in the FS. They are generally of two types:

- Analytical procedures
- Other procedures

Model for an audit plan:

- Agree opening balances to last year's working papers
- Review general ledger for unusual records/transactions
- Check client schedule to/from accounting records/FS
- Carry out analytical review
- Test transactions in detail
- Test balances in detail
- Review presentation and disclosure in the FS

Directional testing

Substantive tests fall into **two categories** (broadly speaking).

- Test to discover **errors** – start **in** the accounting records
- Tests to discover **omissions** – start **outside** of the accounting records

Analytical procedures: the analysis of plausible relationships among financial and non-financial data.

ISA (UK) 520, *Analytical Procedures* gives guidance.

Analytical procedures

Comparisons of this year's financial information with:

- Similar information for prior periods
- Anticipated results/budgets
- Industry information

Consideration of relationships, eg,

- Elements of financial information which are **expected to conform** to patterns
- **Links** between financial/non-financial information

Sources of information

- Interim financial information
- Budget/management accounts
- Non-financial information
- Bank records/VAT returns
- Board minutes
- Discussions with directors

Use of the work of internal audit

ISA (UK) 610 permits external auditors to use the work of internal auditors.

Assessment of internal audit	
Objectivity	Consider the **status** of the function within the entity, who they **report** to, whether they have any **conflicting responsibilities** or **restrictions** placed on their function. Consider also to what extent management acts on internal audit **recommendations**.
Competence	Consider whether internal auditors have adequate **resources**, **technical training** and **proficiency**, and whether internal auditors possess the **required knowledge** of financial reporting. Consider also whether the internal auditors are **members of professional bodies**.
Systematic and disciplined approach	Consider whether internal audit is **properly planned, supervised, reviewed** and **documented**, whether the function has appropriate **quality control procedures**, audit manuals, **work programmes** and **documentation**.

Remember that **the external auditor has sole responsibility for the audit opinion** in the auditor's report.

Types of internal audit work

- Testing of the operating effectiveness of controls
- Substantive procedures involving limited judgement
- Observations of inventory counts
- Tracing transactions through the information system relevant to financial reporting
- Testing of compliance with regulatory requirements
- In some circumstances, audits or reviews of the financial information of subsidiaries

Evaluating specific internal audit work

Consider whether:

- The work was properly planned, performed, supervised, reviewed and documented
- Sufficient, appropriate evidence was obtained to enable the internal auditors to draw reasonable conclusions
- Conclusions reached are appropriate and reports are consistent with the work performed

Using the work of an auditor's expert

ISA (UK) 620 recognises that the need for expertise may arise in fields other than audit and accountancy, for example:

- Valuations of complex financial instruments
- Actuarial calculations
- Estimation of oil and gas reserves
- Valuation of environmental liabilities
- Interpretation of contracts, laws and regulations
- Analysis of complex tax compliance

The auditor who uses an auditor's expert still has sole responsibility for the audit opinion.

Other auditors (in a group)

Component: an entity whose financial information is included in the group financial statements.

Component auditors: auditors who perform work on financial information related to a component of the group audit.

Group engagement team: the auditors with responsibility for performing work on the consolidation process, communicating with component auditors and reporting on the group financial statements.

As well as being responsible for the audit opinion for the group, and for conducting the audit in accordance with legal and regulatory requirements, the group engagement partner is responsible for:

- Understanding the component auditor
- Responding to assessed risks
- Communication with the component auditor
- Evaluating the sufficiency and appropriateness of audit evidence obtained

Main types of estimate

- Inventory obsolescence
- Depreciation of property and equipment
- Valuation of financial instruments
- Outcome of pending litigation
- Fair value of assets or liabilities acquired in a business combination, including the determination of goodwill and intangible assets
- Impairment of long-lived assets, property or equipment held for disposal
- Non-monetary exchanges of assets or liabilities between independent parties
- Revenue recognised for long-term contracts

(ISA (UK) 540: para. A1)

Audit considerations

- Method used
- Relevant controls
- Whether management has used an expert
- The underlying assumptions
- Any change in method from prior period
- Effect of estimation uncertainty

Practical issues

The audit strategy in general will also address practical issues:

- Selecting the right audit team
- Budgets and deadlines
- Timing of interim and final audits
- Location(s) of client premises
- Nature of evidence required

11: Audits of different types of entity

Topic List

Charities

Public sector audits

Some entities do not operate for the purpose of making profit but have other objectives. These not-for-profit entities include charities and public sector bodies.

External and internal auditors might both have to carry out work in not-for-profit organisations. This chapter points out some special considerations when auditing such entities.

The auditing methods you have learned in the rest of your studies are still relevant to these types of audits: these are **additional** *considerations.*

Example

A **charity** is a common form of not-for-profit organisation.

A charity is an institution established for charitable purposes under the Charities Act 2016.

Charitable purposes include:

- Relief of poverty
- Advancement of education
- Advancement of religion
- Purposes to benefit community

Accounts may include:

- Statement of financial activities (SOFA)
- In some cases a summary income and expenditure account
- Balance sheet showing the assets, liabilities and funds of the charity
- Cash flow statement
- Notes

Problem areas	Planning	Inherent risk

Problem areas

- **Donations** (not supported by invoice/equivalent documentation)
- **Legacies** (income recognition)
- **Grants** (often subject to conditions)
- **Restricted funds** (uses are restricted as per deed/ benefactor)
- **Grants to beneficiaries** (must be *bona fide*)
- **Branches** (charities' SORP requires inclusions in main accounts)

Planning

Auditors should consider:

- The **scope** of the audit
- Recommendations of **charity regulators**
- **Accounting policies**
- **Changes in the sector** in which the charity operates
- **Past experience** of the system
- **Key audit areas**
- **Detail** in FS on which auditors report
- **Risk**

Inherent risk

Factors include: complexity/extent of regulation, significance of donations and cash receipts, lack of predictable income, restricted funds, restrictions imposed by charity's governing documents, tax rules, sensitivity of key statistics, balance of maintaining resources/building up funds.

Control risk

Factors include: time committed and degree of involvement by trustees, skills of trustees, independence of trustees from each other, division of duties.

Control environment: segregation of duties a very key area in small charities.

Internal controls

Two key problems

- Lack of segregation of duties
- Use of unqualified staff

Example

Controls over cash donations

Source	Examples of controls
Collecting boxes and tins	■ Numerical control over boxes and tins ■ Satisfactory sealing of boxes and tins so that any opening prior to recording cash is apparent ■ Regular collecting and recording of proceeds ■ Dual control over counting and recording of proceeds
Postal receipts	■ Unopened mail kept securely ■ Dual control over the opening of mail ■ Immediate recording of donations on opening of mail or receipt ■ Agreement of bank paying-in slips to record of receipts by an independent person

Audit evidence

- Consider **understatement/incompleteness** in **income**
- **Overstatement of grants or assets**
- Misanalysis or misuse of **funds**
- Misstatement of assets like **donated properties**
- Existence of restricted funds in foreign **branches**

Reporting

The form of the auditor's report is dictated by the charity's constitution but it should conform to ISA (UK) 700 criteria. The financial statements should have been prepared in accordance with any charities legislation, so that fact should be referred to in the auditor's report.

Where charities are not governed by statute, the auditor's report will depend upon the scope of the assignment.

Overall review

Consider if **accounting policies** are appropriate. **Analytical procedures** might be restricted due to lack of predictable income etc, but charities should have budget or strategy information available.

Features of public sector audit

- Financial statements
- Internal controls
- Regularity
- Propriety
- Value for money

Principles of public sector audit

- Accountability for public funds
- Independence of auditors
- Wide scope of audit
- Results of audit available to public

Value for money

- Economy (spend less)
- Efficiency (spend well)
- Effectiveness (spend wisely)

ISAs (UK) apply to audit work undertaken in the public sector. A number of ISAs contain considerations specific to public sector entities.

Internal audit in the public sector

Internal audit is a statutory requirement in many parts of the public sector.

> **Internal audit:** an independent, objective assurance and consulting activity designed to add value and improve an organisation's operations.

The code of ethics for internal auditors in the public sector contains four principles covering:

- Integrity
- Objectivity
- Confidentiality
- Competency

Public Sector Internal Audit Standards (PSIAS) come under the general headings of:

- Attribute standards – purpose of IA, independence, proficiency and quality assurance.
- Performance standards – management, planning, performance, communication, monitoring etc.

Notes

12: Audit completion

Topic List

Financial statements review

Going concern

Subsequent events

In this chapter we discuss the significance of the going concern concept and the importance of the auditor's going concern review. If the going concern basis is not appropriate, the financial statements will be materially affected.

The post year end period is vital for the auditor in obtaining audit evidence. ISA (UK) 560 outlines audit guidance regarding subsequent events.

We also discuss the importance of the overall review of the financial statements.

Financial statements review | Going concern | Subsequent events

Towards the end of their audit, the auditors should review the financial statements to ensure that they are reasonable, and consistent with evidence obtained, so that they can draw a conclusion on truth and fairness.

Do the financial statements comply with the Companies Act 2006?

A firm's audit pack should contain a checklist to ensure that disclosure requirements are met. The issue is complex because:

- There are a large number of financial reporting standards.
- The Companies Act itself is a substantial document that determines the format to be used.
- The directors' report etc needs to be consistent with the financial statements.

Do the financial statements make sense?

Analytical procedures must be used at the end of the audit when forming an overall conclusion. There are three steps involved:

1 Interpretation – of the figures and ratios in the FS.

2 Investigation – of potential problems identified; solutions should have been found by the completion stage.

3 Corroboration – where further work needs to be carried out and any necessary amendments to the FS are actioned.

| Financial statements review | Going concern | Subsequent events |

When financial statements are prepared on a going concern basis, assets and liabilities are recorded on the basis that they can be realised and discharged in the normal course of business. The alternative is the 'liquidation' basis.

Going concern basis of accounting: the financial statements are prepared on the assumption that the entity is a going concern and will continue its operations for the foreseeable future. This is the case unless management either intends to liquidate the entity or to cease operations, or has no realistic alternative but to do so.

(ISA (UK) 570: para. 2)

ISA (UK) 570, *Going Concern* gives guidance.

Auditor responsibilities

The auditor's responsibilities are to obtain sufficient appropriate audit evidence regarding, and conclude on:

- Whether a material uncertainty related to going concern exists; and
- The appropriateness of management's use of the going concern basis of accounting in the preparation of the financial statements.

(ISA (UK) 570: paras. 6–1)

Risk assessment procedures and related activities

In obtaining an understanding of the entity, the auditor shall design and perform risk assessment procedures. If management have undertaken a preliminary assessment of going concern, the auditor shall review it. The auditor shall remain alert throughout the audit for any factors which would indicate problems (examples given below).

Examples

Financial

- Net liabilities
- Fixed term borrowing approaching maturity without realistic prospect of renewal/repayment
- Negative operating cash flows
- Adverse financial ratios
- Substantial operation losses
- Inability to pay creditors
- Inability to finance new products

Operating

- Loss of key management/markets/franchise
- Labour difficulties/supply shortage

Other

- Major legal proceedings/non-compliance

Completion stage

Consider indications of:

- Receivables unable to pay
- Inventory NRV less than cost
- Assets no longer usable
- Irrecoverable development expenditure
- Investments losing value

Further procedures – review

- Future business plans, forecasts, projections
- Adequacy of borrowing facilities
- Minutes and other indicators of going concern

Financial statements review	Going concern	Subsequent events

Reporting

GC assumption appropriate, no material uncertainties → 'Conclusions relating to going concern' section, unmodified report

GC assumption appropriate but a material uncertainty exists.

Adequately disclosed → Unmodified opinion with Material Uncertainty Related to Going Concern paragraph (ISA (UK) 570 provides example)

Inadequate disclosure → Qualified opinion

GC assumption **inappropriate** → **Adverse opinion**

Management unwilling to extend assessment → Qualified opinion/Disclaimer

Subsequent events are events occurring between the date of the financial statements and the date of the auditor's report, and facts that become known to the auditor after the date of the auditor's report. There are two types: those that provide evidence of conditions that existed at the date of the FS (**adjusting events**) and those that provide evidence of conditions that arose after the date of the FS (**non-adjusting events**).

Adjusting events

- Resolution of court case
- Bankruptcy of major customer
- Evidence of NRV of inventories
- Discovery of fraud

Non-adjusting events

- Destruction of asset by flood or fire
- Major share transactions
- Announcement of plans to close part of business
- Dividends proposed after end of reporting period

Prior to the auditor's report being signed

Auditors must carry out audit procedures to obtain evidence about subsequent events, including:

Audit procedures

- Enquiries of management
- Reading minutes of meetings of those charged with governance
- Reviewing most recent financial information

Examples: enquiries of management

What is the status of items involving subjective data included in the FS?

Are there any new commitments (borrowing/guarantees) in the new year?

Have there been any issues of capital?

Have there been any major events?

Are there any unusual accounting treatment adjustments?

After the date of the auditor's report the auditor has no responsibility for further work but may have to act if material facts come to be known.

13: Reporting

Topic List

Reports to management

Audit opinion

Auditor's report

It is crucial that you are aware of different types of auditor's reports before you take the exam. Past exam questions will give you an idea of the scenarios that could come up.

Communication with those charged with governance

Guidance on reporting to management and other non-shareholders as a by-product of audit is given in ISA (UK) 260, *Communication with Those Charged with Governance.*

Governance is the term used to describe the role of persons entrusted with the supervision, control and direction of the entity. Those charged with governance are ordinarily accountable for ensuring that the entity achieves its objectives, financial reporting and reporting to interested parties. Those charged with governance include management **only** when it performs such functions.

Matters shall be discussed with those charged with governance on a **sufficiently prompt basis** so that they can react to what the auditor has said. The auditor should determine who those charged with governance are.

If an **audit committee** exists, it is likely to be the appropriate body to report matters arising from the audit to. Such relevant matters are outlined here.

Matters to be communicated (ISA (UK) 260)

- The auditor's responsibility in relation to FS audit
- Planned scope and timing of the audit
- Auditor independence
- Significant findings, including:
  - Qualitative aspects of accounting practice
  - Significant difficulties encountered
  - Significant matters discussed with management

ISA (UK) 265 requires auditors to report on significant deficiencies in internal control. Matters to consider include:

- Likelihood of material misstatement
- Susceptibility to loss or fraud
- Amounts, volumes and importance of controls to financial reporting

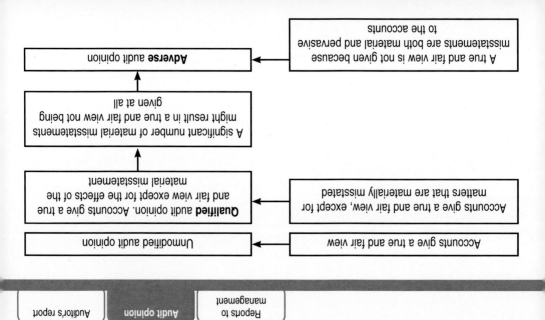

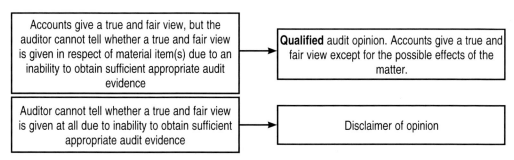

Accounts give a true and fair view, but the auditor cannot tell whether a true and fair view is given in respect of material item(s) due to an inability to obtain sufficient appropriate audit evidence → **Qualified** audit opinion. Accounts give a true and fair view except for the possible effects of the matter.

Auditor cannot tell whether a true and fair view is given at all due to inability to obtain sufficient appropriate audit evidence → Disclaimer of opinion

Emphasis of matter paragraph

An auditor may wish to include an emphasis of matter paragraph, eg, when the financial statements are affected by a fundamental uncertainty such as the recoverability of a receivables balance, or the potential incurring of a liability such as a fine.

If the financial statements contain disclosure about the matter, the auditor will **not** modify his opinion, but may wish to use the auditor's report to draw attention to the matter in the accounts.

The process of forming an audit opinion in an exam can be summarised in a step format, as follows:

1 Read through all the information given in the question carefully and analyse the requirement.

2 Read through the information given in the question again in the light of the requirement, making notes of any key factors.

3 Ascertain whether all the evidence reasonably expected to be available has been obtained and evaluated.

4 If not, identify whether the effect of not gaining evidence is such that the financial statements could as a whole be misleading (disclaimer of opinion) or in material part could be misleading (qualified opinion).

5 Ascertain whether the financial statements have been prepared in accordance with generally accepted accounting principles (GAAP).

6 If not, determine whether departure was required to give a true and fair view and if so, whether it has been properly disclosed.

7 Decide whether any unnecessary departure is material to the financial statements (qualifed opinion) or is pervasive to them (adverse opinion).

8 Conclude whether the financial statements as a whole give a true and fair view.

Even if the answers to steps 3 and 5 are yes, you must still carry out step 8 and make an overall assessment of the truth and fairness of the financial statements in order to conclude that an unmodified opinion is appropriate.

Contents of auditor's report – ISA (UK) 700

- Title
- Addressee
- Auditor's opinion
- Basis for opinion
- Going concern
- Key audit matters
- Other information
- Responsibilities for the financial statements
- Auditor's responsibilities
- Other reporting responsibilities
- Name of the engagement partner
- Signature of the auditor
- Auditor's address
- Date

Merits of the auditor's report

- The report clearly spells out **to whom** the report is **addressed**
- The report clearly states the **financial statements** it refers to
- The report refers to the **respective responsibilities** of directors/auditors
- It outlines the **process** of auditing
- It explains the audit opinion
- The opinion is prominent at the start of the report, improving clarity and understandability

Criticisms of the auditor's report

- Steps taken are insufficient and the report is **not clear** to a non-financial investor
- The report includes incomprehensible **audit jargon**
  - True and fair
  - Materiality
- Description of audit **unclear**
- Extent of management responsibility not clear

Reports to management

Audit opinion

Auditor's report

14: Other assurance engagements

For other types of assurance engagement it is important to agree the terms with the client.

If a firm is appointed, for example, to review a cash flow forecast that a client has prepared to support an attempt to raise finance from a bank, there are further issues to consider and to include in the engagement letter:

- The intended use of the information
- Whether the information will be for general or limited distribution
- The nature of the assumptions, that is whether they are best-estimate or hypothetical assumptions
- The elements to be included in the information
- The period covered by the information
- A caveat warning that there could be differences between the forecast and actual performance due to unforeseen circumstances

Assurance report

Less formal than auditor's report

Reasonable or limited assurance

Notes

Notes